Run Away and Hide

Hiding

"Kids 3 to 8"

Jessie Eldora Robertson

Inquiries and Book Orders should be addressed to:

Great Writers Media
Email: info@greatwritersmedia.com
Phone: 877-600-5469

ISBN: 978-1-959493-80-8 (sc)
ISBN: 978-1-959493-81-5 (hc)
ISBN: 978-1-959493-79-2 (ebk)

Dedication

To my sweet little great granddaughter,
Aria Grace who's being, is a joy in my life.

A story for now and a story book towards her future.

Aria has just turned four years old. She loves to play even more now. "Is that possible, playing more?" She is always making funny faces. Everyday Aria plays hide & seek, but … it is not the planned game. Aria puts Mommy & Grammy to the chase. The longest arms get to reach for her. Aria is a "tease", she always has been a "tease." And, at a contrast, "Is this when arguing begins?" The story will take you to Aria's hiding places all around the house and outside too, and in the summer and the winter. You will see her funny faces. "Oh, she likes to cuddle too." Enjoy the ventures in the days of little Aria.

Enjoy this picture book!

About The Author

The Author continues to do freelance photography and writing. Jessie is self taught and a self starter in many areas of her talents. Jessie Eldora Robertson is published on Online Photography stock sites:

Shutterstock, Getty Images and Dreamstime. Published writing works include Anthologies in poetry books. She has edited her late husband's book - finally, in 2022: The Autobody Repair Man by George L. Phillips. Published (to date) is her own Memoir, first edition; a revised edition - Working like A Man.

Little Aria lives with the author, her (Great) Grammy Jessie, Granddad Bill and Mommy Brittany in the Cariboo Chilcotin in the city of Williams Lake, British Columbia, Canada.

This book belongs to:

_____

Aria is 4 years old
And loves to play
Hiding is her Game

When Aria was little
Her spot was hiding in the toy box
Beside her stuffys

I don't want to go to bed just yet
I'll hide under the kitchen table

I run away to hide
Under the doggy
So big and furry

Mommy came by
And found me
With doggy so pretty

Running around the tree

Makes me so happy

Mommy will wonder where I will be

I hide under the table
By the Christmas tree
But I know everyone can see me!

I dug a hole in the snow … to hide away
To deep for anyone to come find me?

Here comes Mommy …
Coming to get me
I'll throw snow at her!

Hiding in the workshop
With toys for playing
Just Grammy and me

I swing on my swing
Having my snow clothes on …
Inside in winter!

I like to snuggle and hide
With my Mommy ...
The couch so soft ... and with blanky

Aria climbs and plays
On Grammy's bed
Tossing in the soft covers

Aria hides under the covers
She won't come out
Until Grammy does discover

I 'll hide under my bed
I don't want to go potty
You can't catch me

I have a special hide to run to
I sit with my tablet
By the gate at the end of the hall

My go-to hiding place …
I can run really fast …
To duck down behind the couch

Hiding in the garden
With all the greenery
With only my grandpa beside me

Then I run over to the Rockery ...
Lots of space to me to run
And find a place to hide

Snuggling in the corner
With stuffy and blanket
I am out of the way of stepping feet

I can brush my hair
All my myself!
And you can't see me

The bunny is running away
To under the back steps
I can't grab him … who's hiding now?

I want to hug Scully the cat
But he doesn't want to
Scully is getting away ...

Where did Scully go?
He jumped up the counter and to the refrigerator
He will stay safe now!

Auntie Leah's ducks
Are moving into a 'huddle' away
What has 'spooked' them today?

Why, it is Aria

The ducks are hiding from …

But there is a fence, so the ducks are safe!

The 3 of us
Mommy, Me, and Grammy – All hiding!

That's me, Aria
I love ice cream
And eating snow … and stickers!

End of my story ☺

Printed in the USA
CPSIA information can be obtained
at www.ICGtesting.com
LVHW060905020224
770600LV00002B/17